# PICK YOUR BRAINS

## about

# ITALY

## Jez Mathews

Illustrations by
Caspar Williams & Craig Dixon

**CADOGAN**

Illustrations by Caspar Williams and Craig Dixon
Illustrations and map copyright © Cadogan Guides 2004
Map by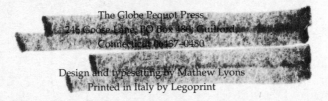

Cadogan Guides
Network House, 1 Ariel Way, London W12 7SL
info@cadoganguides.co.uk
www.cadoganguides.com

The Globe Pequot Press
246 Goose Lane, PO Box 480, Guilford
Connecticut 06437–0480

Design and typesetting by Mathew Lyons
Printed in Italy by Legoprint

# Contents

Not to scale!

# Vital Facts
# and Figures

**Population:** 57.4 million.

**Capital:** Rome (population: 2.7 million).

**Other major cities by population:** Milan (4.25 million), Naples (3 million), Turin (1.3 million).

**Other great cities:** Bologna, Florence, Genoa, Trieste, Venice.

**Regions:** Abruzzo; Basilicata; Calabria; Campania; Emilia Romagna; Friuli-Venezia-Giulia; Lazio; Liguria; Marche; Lombardy; Molise; Piedmont; Puglia; Sardinia; Sicily; Trentino-Alto Adige; Tuscany; Umbria; Valle D'Aosta; Veneto.

Italy is intensely regional. People consider themselves as Florentines or Romans (if they come from Florence or Rome, for example) before they think of themselves as Italians. The leading newspaper, *La Repubblica*, has separate editions in Rome, Naples, Bologna and Milan to cater for all the local news that people want to read!

**Size:** Italy has an area of 187,123 square kilometres (116,273 square miles). It is 1,300 km (808 miles) long, north to south.

**Borders:** Austria, France, Slovenia and Switzerland. Technically, it also has borders with the two independent principalities within its boundaries – the Vatican City and San Marino.

**Coasts:** Italy has 7,500 km (4,660 miles) of coastline. It has the Ligurian Sea and the Tyrrhenian Sea to the west; the Ionian Sea to the south; and the Adriatic to the east.

**Mountains:** Italy shares the Alps with Austria, France and Switzerland. The Apennines run down the length of the country.

**Volcanoes:** There are six areas of volcanic activity – Mount Etna on Sicily; Stromboli and Vulcano in the Aeolian Islands; and Vesuvius, the Phlegrean Fields and the island of Ischia near Naples. Vesuvius is causing particular concern at the moment. It normally erupts every 30 years, but hasn't done so since 1944.

**Highest point:** Mont Blanc in the Alps is 4,807 metres (15,770 ft) high. The highest peak in the Apennines is the Corno Grande at 2,914 metres (9,560 ft).

**Rivers:** The Po is the longest river in Italy, starting in the Alps and emptying into the Adriatic. The other main rivers are the Arno through Florence and the Tiber through Rome.

**Lakes:** There are three great lakes in Italy – Maggiore, Como and Garda – all in the north. Lombardy has Lake Como to itself, but shares Maggiore with Piedmont and Garda with both Trentino-Alto Adige and Veneto.

**Major ports:** Genoa, Venice, Trieste, Palermo, Naples, La Spezia.

**Islands:** there are many islands in Italy. The most well known are Sicily, Sardinia, Capri and Elba.

**Terrain:** The Italian countryside is rugged and mountainous, dominated by the Apennines. Only about a quarter of its total area is lowland plain. The most fertile region is that around the River Po in the north.

**Distances:** Rome is 1,175 km (730 miles) from Berlin; 6,180 km (3,840 miles) from Bombay; 8,449 km (5,250 miles) from Cape Town; 9,286 km (5,770 miles) from Hong Kong; 1,432 km (890 miles) from London; 10,187 km (6,330 miles) from Los Angeles; 15,981 km (9,930 miles) from Melbourne; 2,366 km (1,470 miles) from Moscow; 6,872 km (4,270 miles) from New York; 1,094 km (680 miles) from Paris; and 9,849 km (6,120 miles) from Tokyo.

**Language:** Italian, although it is only in the last few decades that Italian has actually been the 'first' language for the majority of Italians. The Italian nation has many regional tongues and dialects which are still used commonly on a daily basis. There are in fact 29 languages currently spoken in Italy, with some having just a few thousand speakers left! The full list is: Albanian (Arbëreshë); Bavarian; Catalan-Valencian-Balear; Cimbrian; Corsican; Emiliano-Romagnolo; Franco-Provençal; Friulian; Greek; Judeo-Italian; Ladin; Ligurian; Lombard; Mócheno; Napoletano-Calabrese; Piedmontese; Provençal; Romani, Balkan; Romani, Sinte; Romani, Vlax; Sardinian, Campidanese; Sardinian, Gallurese; Sardinian, Logudorese; Sardinian, Sassarese; Serbo-Croatian; Sicilian; Slovenian; Venetian; and Walser.

German is also spoken up near the Swiss and Austrian borders, as is French in Piedmont and Valle d'Aosta.

**Italian dialects**: There are two major groups of Italian dialects, separated north and south by the Spezia-Rimini line. To the north are the Septentrional dialects: Gallo-Italic and Venetic. To the south are the Centro-Meridionale dialects: Tuscan, Latin-Umbrian-Marchegian, Intermediate Meridional and Extreme Meridional.

**Major religion:** About 98% of the population is Roman Catholic. However, there are well-established Protestant and Jewish communities and a growing number of Muslims.

**Monetary unit:** 1 Euro = approximately 66 pence or 142 US cents.

**Heritage currency:** the Lira. This word derives from the Latin word *'libra'*, meaning 'pound'. The £ UK currency symbol is actually a corrupted L-shape, referring back to the same root. Lire first made their appearance in Venice in 1472 and were adopted as the national currency when the Italian state was born in 1861. However, its value was significantly lower than other European currencies thanks to the country's periodic economic problems. A typical exchange rate in the years leading up to the adoption of the Euro might have been as much as 2,000 Lire to every £1.

**Main exports:** a wealth of food and wine, machinery, cars and transport equipment, fashion, furniture and design.

**Internet domain:** .it

**Opening hours:** Shops are usually open from 9am to 7.30pm, with a lunch break from 1pm to 3.30pm (Monday – Saturday). Banks open at 8.30am until 1.30pm (Monday – Friday) and from 3.30pm to 4.30pm (Monday – Thursday). According to a recent survey, there are three times as many shops per person in Italy than in

Britain – and twice as many cafés and restaurants.

**Television:** There is one TV set for every 2.3 people.

**Art:** Some 60% of the world's most important works of art are located in Italy. Of these, a staggering 50% are in Florence.

**Water:** Italians don't like tap water very much. They drink more mineral water than any other people in Europe!

**Pasta consumption:** The average Italian eats 28kg (61.6 lbs) of pasta every year. This is nothing compared to the average Sicilian, however, who eats 42kg (92.4 lbs).

**On the road:** Driving is on the right. You have to be 18 and over to drive a car. The maximum speed limit on the motorways is 129km (80mph). Seat belts must be worn in the front of a car and in the back. Children under 12 have to sit in the rear. Braking isn't something that comes naturally to Italian drivers, so

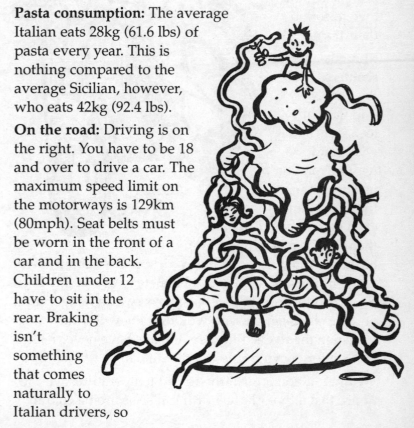

tourists always have a little adjustment to do, as the Italians like to drive quite fast! However, any shyness with the brakes is more than made up for with their enthusiasm for the horn. The Italians love to sound their horns!

**Mopeds and scooters:** They are hugely popular with teenagers and with good reason. You don't need a driving test to ride one and – even better – you can take them on the road from your fourteenth birthday. You will see as many girls as boys about town on their mopeds. True, crash helmets have recently been made compulsory, and you can't carry a passenger until you are eighteen, but you wouldn't know it from watching the roads. But then, Italians have never really gone in for obeying rules all that much!

**Weather:** If you look at the record temperatures, you'll notice that although the north can see extreme cold in

## Record temperatures (º centigrade)

|  | low | high |
|---|---|---|
| ☞ Bologna | -19 | 41 |
| ☞ Florence | -23 | 43 |
| ☞ Genoa | -8 | 40 |
| ☞ Milan | -18 | 39 |
| ☞ Naples | -7 | 40 |
| ☞ Rome | -11 | 41 |
| ☞ Trieste | -16 | 37 |
| ☞ Turin | -21 | 41 |
| ☞ Venice | -13 | 38 |

winter, the highest summer temperatures don't vary that much across the country. August in Italy can be unbearably hot, which is why most of the country goes on holiday that month. The best time of year to visit is often in late spring or early autumn, unless you are keen on winter sports in the Italian Alps.

Also, it's easy to assume that Italian weather is almost always fantastic. And of course it is – most of the time. But it still varies too. In Rome there is a hot, wet wind from the south called a Scirocco. Even Venice, arguably the most beautiful city in the world, has more than its share of rain.

# Italian History in a Nutshell

I f you go back far enough, all history begins with tribes. Four thousand years ago in Italy, you might have come across some of these on your travels: the Ligurians, Siculi, Sards, Umbrii, Veneti and Latins. Recognize any of them? That you can still see their names on the map today tells you a lot about Italian history – and reminds you just how recent the creation of a single Italian nation was (1861, by the way.)

## Bronze Age

Italian history really begins around 1,000 years BC. People came to settle here from all over the Mediterranean: the Phoenicians came from what is now the Lebanon; the Carthaginians from Tunisia; the Celts from France; and the Greeks from, well, Greece. No one knows where the Etruscans came from. You can probably guess where they settled, though.

## The Greeks in Italy

Greek civilization had a strong foothold in southern Italy, which was known as *Magna Graecia* (Greater

Greece). It included all of modern Calabria and a great deal of modern Sicily, Puglia, Basilicata and Campania. It was established in the eighth century BC but was already in decline a few hundred years later. Most people don't realize that many scenes from Greek myth and legend are actually set in Italy. The entrance to Hades, the Underworld, was in what the Greeks called the Phlegrean Fields just a few miles around the bay from Naples. You can still visit this scary area of volcanic activity today – a must if you like the stench of sulphur and boiling mud pits!

The great writer Homer, who wrote the story of Troy, also wrote of Ulysses coming here in his book *The Odyssey*. The hero negotiated his way between the sea monsters of Scylla and Charybdis in the straits of Messina, which separate Sicily from the mainland, and was tempted by two water nymphs, known as the

Sirens, on Campanella Point on the peninsula of Sorrento, looking out to the island of Capri. It is said that, when Ulysses refused to listen to their songs and sailed away, one of the Sirens, Parthenope, was so distraught that she died of a broken heart. A city bearing her name was built around her tomb. That city is now known as Naples. Her tomb is rumoured to lie beneath the Teatro San Carlo, the great Neapolitan opera house (which, incidentally, is the biggest opera house in Italy).

---

### *Where to see Magna Graecia*

You can see the traces of Magna Graecia all over southern Italy. But among the best preserved sites are:

☞ The valley of the temples at Agrigento in Sicily.

☞ The Temple of Neptune at Paestum, just outside Salerno in Campania. There are two other temples here, as well as a superb museum, but the Temple of Neptune is the most complete.

## Rome – Not Built in a Day

Rome would begin its long march to world domination as an Etruscan town. However, in 509 BC, the Romans threw off their shackles and declared themselves a republic. Over the next few centuries, Rome would overrun Etruria, invade the rich Greek-controlled areas in the south and defeat the Carthaginians in a series of battles, which have gone down in history as the Punic Wars. The most famous of these involved Hannibal, the legendary Carthaginian general, marching his army and its elephants over the Alps and into Italy from the north. The Romans, who had been expecting an attack from the south, were completely taken by surprise.

Caligula and Nero have gone down in history as two of the most brutal and eccentric Roman emperors ever.

### Caligula

When Caligula began his reign, he seemed quite normal but, within months, a serious illness had unhinged his mind. He declared himself a god and insisted that statues of himself be erected for the Romans to worship. He kept his favourite racehorse, Incitatus, in an ivory stable in the imperial palace. Dinner guests were surprised to find their invitations were actually from the horse – and even more surprised when it joined them at the table! Caligula even made his horse a consul. Once, on a military expedition, his army was ordered to collect seashells from the beaches to mark Caligula's 'conquest' of the sea! The army was none too happy.

Caligula was an unusually hairy man. He said he would execute anyone who mentioned goats in his presence!

## Nero

Nero fancied himself as a great artist. He often entered dramatic competitions – which he was always allowed to win!

Although he is best remembered for playing a fiddle as Rome burned, this isn't wholly accurate: the violin wouldn't be invented for centuries. But, when a fire destroyed much of Rome in AD 64, he did write a song about it while he watched! The Romans were so angry with his attitude that it was rumoured that Nero lit the fires just to see what Troy might have looked like in flames. (Nero himself blamed the Christians.)

But perhaps the Romans were right about Nero. The fire enabled him to buy a vast area in the centre of Rome to build himself a palace, which was to be coated in solid gold. For that reason, it was known as the Golden House, or Domus Aurea, and you can still visit its ruins in Rome today.

In any event, Nero certainly wasn't a safe man to have around. He murdered his mother and his wife within a year or two of taking power.

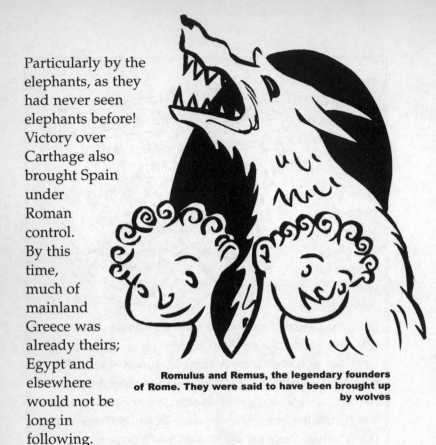

Particularly by the elephants, as they had never seen elephants before! Victory over Carthage also brought Spain under Roman control. By this time, much of mainland Greece was already theirs; Egypt and elsewhere would not be long in following.

**Romulus and Remus, the legendary founders of Rome. They were said to have been brought up by wolves**

## Rome – Decline and Fall

Having extraordinary wealth had its problems. Rome was torn apart by great rivalries, which became so bad that the army had to seize control. Eventually, the role of emperor was created. But by the end of the second century AD, the empire was a victim of its own success. Emperor Diocletian divided it into two halves, with the eastern half governed from Byzantium.

Byzantium – the modern day Istanbul – was the gateway between Asia and Europe. It became the richest and greatest city in the world. Rome, meanwhile, grew weaker each year.

## The Dark Ages

Towards the end of the fourth century, Rome had become so feeble that it was unable to defend itself against the armies of Ostrogoths, Vandals, Visigoths and Huns, who launched themselves against it from Russia, Hungary and elsewhere. In 410, the city fell.

The next centuries were difficult. Byzantium reclaimed the Italian peninsula for the Eastern Empire, but failed to hold on to it. The Lombards, a Germanic tribe, were pushing down into the north. The Normans conquered Sicily and elsewhere in the south. In fact, they first landed in Sicily at Messina in 1061 and some of the Norman knights who fought there would go onto to fight at Hastings in 1066.

Charlemagne, King of the Franks (a Germanic people) and one of the greatest European leaders, added most of the country to his Carolingian Empire. The Church in Rome, now well adrift from the remains of the old empire in Byzantium and presumably despairing of everyone else, began building its own political power. In 738, it created a Holy Roman Empire of its own in opposition to that in the East and made Charlemagne its first emperor. Sadly, his dynasty would fail. But the Holy Roman Empire would live on.

## Warrior Popes

Italy entered the second millennium weak and divided. The pope was constantly arguing with the emperor over who was most powerful. Emperors resented their interference – some violently, some very violently!

This was a scary dispute as papal power was real: it was not unknown for popes to lead armies into battle. Take one such pope, Julius II. It is said that Michelangelo was creating a life-size bronze sculpture and suggested that Julius stand with one hand raised and the other holding a book. 'A book?,' replied Julius. 'What do I know about books? Just put a sword in it.' The disagreement spread across Italy for the first two centuries of the new millennium, dividing the country down the middle: those who supported the pope were known as Guelphs, those who stood by the emperor were known as Ghibellines.

You can get a sense of the dispute even today in Tuscany. Florence, a Guelph city, was all for trade and commerce. Compare how it feels to walk around there to walking in the more medieval, feudal, Ghibelline city of Siena.

---
*Things were different then!*

In the ninth century, there was an English pope called John VIII. It is said that one day he was riding through Rome when, to everyone's astonishment, he got off his horse, sat down by the roadside and gave birth to a baby. John was actually a woman called Joan!

24

## Trading Up

Weak and divided it may have been, but Italy became the wealthiest country in Europe, capitalizing on the superb geographical position that had attracted the Phoenicians and others 2,000 years earlier to control the trade routes around the Mediterranean and out of the East. They were also brilliant negotiators and deal-makers. The Venetians even persuaded the Fourth Crusade not to reclaim Jerusalem for Christianity but to attack Constantinople instead, the Christian capital of the Byzantine Empire – and more importantly Venice's main rival for trade!

The argument between Guelphs and Ghibellines wasn't just about the power of the Pope. It was also about commerce. The papacy, as the Catholic Church in Rome is known, supported the new independent states, such as Florence, Milan, Naples, Venice and Genoa, whereas the Empire wished to keep all political power to itself.

However, the centuries that saw endless feuding

between the city states also witnessed the great cultural triumph of the Renaissance – the 'rebirth' of European art and civilisation – from Dante in the thirteenth century to Michelangelo in the sixteenth century. One reason for this is that life inside the cities was relatively peaceful. Much of the real fighting took place between armies of *condottieri* (mercenaries) outside the cities. The situation suited everyone apart from the poor peasants caught in the middle!

## Spanish Steps

Elsewhere in Europe, nation states, such as France and Spain, were emerging and Italian cities began forming alliances with them. Soon the Italian peninsula was swarming with French, Spanish, German and Swiss armies, all impressed with the wealth and vulnerability of their increasingly nervous hosts. Matters came to a head when Charles V succeeded to the Spanish throne in 1516. Not a man to do things by halves, within three years he had taken control of the Holy Roman Empire and soon began to turn his eye to Italy. By 1530, almost all of it was his. In 1527 his army had even sacked Rome. This had big consequences for English history, since the pope felt it unwise – as Charles's prisoner, more or less – to let Henry VIII's wriggle out of his marriage to Catherine of Aragon, who just happened

## Garibaldi: the great Italian hero

Garibaldi's efforts to liberate Italy made him famous –
and a hero – the world over. When he visited London in
1864, over 600,000 people thronged the streets to catch
a glimpse of him. He was even invited to inspect the
British fleet.

to be Charles V's aunt. As a result, Henry went on to
create a Protestant Church of England, which would
enable him to do as he wanted.

## Independent Daze

For the next 300 years, Italy would be under Spanish,
Austrian or French control (Napoleon even briefly
crowned himself King of Italy). But by the middle of the
nineteenth century, the nation was ready for change. A
movement for Italian independence, reform and
unification was born. It was called the Risorgimento and
was led by Giuseppe Garibaldi, one of the great heroes
of modern-day Italy. It may have taken him 30 years to
succeed, but succeed he did, formally establishing a
kingdom of Italy in 1861 – although it would be another
10 years before it included the two great cities of Rome
and Venice. The trade wasn't all one-way, however:
Nice, now on the French Riviera, was Italian up to this
point. Unfortunately, the new kingdom wasn't good for
everyone. While the north modernized and became
more like the rest of industrial northern Europe, the
south slipped back into a kind of feudal poverty.

## Modern Italy

The Italians fought alongside England and France in
the First World War and their defeat of the Austrians at
the battle of Vittorio Veneto is celebrated in the street
names of every city and town throughout Italy. But the
war had crippled Italy financially and the ensuing
social unrest gave the Fascist leader Benito Mussolini
the opportunity to seize power for himself by declaring
a dictatorship in 1925.

Mussolini then led Italy into the Second World War
on the side of Hitler's Nazi Germany.

The Allies landed in Sicily in 1943 and fought their
way up the peninsula for the next 18 months. When
defeat was inevitable, Mussolini tried to escape to
Switzerland but was caught by the Italian Resistance in
April 1945 and shot.

## Since 1946

Italy declared itself a republic in 1946. The country has
seen over 60 governments since the war (by comparison,
Britain has had 11). Despite that – or, maybe because of it
– Italy has prospered as never before.

# Local Customs: How the Italians Live

## Meeting and Greeting

In Spain and Austria it's always two, starting on the right cheek. In the Netherlands, too, you begin on the right but are allowed three. The French always start on the left but can go for anything between two and six, depending on which part of the country you are in. What are we on about? Why, the greeting kiss, of course!

Unlike other continental European countries, there are no strict rules about this in Italy. It doesn't really matter which cheek you start with – the confusion is part of the fun – and two is the usual number, although young people increasingly go for three. In general, it's only family or close friends who you kiss (we're talking air kisses here by the way). The right way to say hello is 'Ciao!', which can handily also mean 'goodbye', thus saving you having to learn another word. Other more formal alternatives to the kiss are the good old British handshake or possibly a hug. Raising your eyebrows a few millimeters and grunting 'Alright?' (as many in the UK do) would not be good!

If all this seems pretty alien, it is worth remembering

that Italy hasn't always been so keen to smooch. Kissing in public was punishable by death in Naples in the sixteenth century.

## Family matters

Italians are famous for their great family tradition and love of family life. The family has always been central to Italian life and still is. Meal times are very important to Italian families and adults and children will spend a long time preparing large family meals that last considerably longer than you might be used to. These are great events and can last for several hours and normally children will stay up much later than you usually do to join in the festivities. It is also quite usual for grandparents to live in the same house with their children and grandchildren. Elderly people are treated with great respect in Italy as are mothers. In fact, 'Mamas' are always strong figures in Italian households and young Italians are much more likely to continue living at home until they are married, than in other countries.

But nothing demonstrates the love of family quite so much as the Italian

love of children. Children, especially babies, are adored throughout Italy. If you have a younger brother or sister you may, when walking down the street, have to stop every three minutes for the baby to be admired! Expect lots of attention, head patting and praise, too – even at your age! And expect, too, to be treated like an adult in restaurants – and indulged even if you don't quite behave like one!

Italian children are taken everywhere with their parents and you will often see children walking around in the evenings much later than you would be allowed to at home or all eating together in restaurants. It is not unknown for restaurants to give bored kids presents to amuse them. Italians are very tolerant of children, but won't be impressed by bad manners. Italian children tend to be quite well behaved.

## A Walk down an Italian Street

The first thing that you will notice when you step out onto the street of an Italian city or visit a small village is the bustle and liveliness of Italy. Italians are an open, expressive and friendly nation who use their hands a great deal to express how they are feeling and to illustrate what they are saying (there are whole books dedicated to Italian hand gestures and what they mean!). Wherever you are in Italy you will often hear neighbours and families chatting loudly to one another across courtyards. The Italians are also stylish, careful dressers! You will notice amazingly brightly coloured clothes and recognize some of the famous Italian designer shops such as Gucci and Benetton. In fact, Italian style and design expertise is world-renowned in everything from furniture to fast cars.

## Italians and their cars

Ah yes, the cars. Italians love their cars, which is no surprise as the Italians make some of the best cars in the world such as Fiat and Lamborghini. In Italy, people use the car horn to say hello to someone along

---

*What Italians think of the Italians!*

Like every country, Italy has its regional stereotypes. These are some of Italy's – but don't take them too seriously! It is jokingly said that the Bolognesi (people who come from Bologna) are self-important; Florentines (people who come from Florence) think they know it all; Milanese (people who come from Milan) have no sense of humour; Neapolitans (from Naples) are extroverts; Sardinians are dreamy.

the street – and just don't stop! But don't mistake this for rudeness. The Italians are incredibly polite and charming people, who find bad manners – however old you are – really shocking. The Italians simply live life how life ought to be lived – loudly and at full speed!

## The Night Before Christmas

In many Italian households, especially in central and southern Italy, it is traditional to cook a large meal on the night of Christmas Eve consisting only of fish dishes, having fasted for 24 hours previously. No one knows why, but the number of dishes you are meant to cook is always an odd one – between 7 and 13 – and varies from region to region.

## Christmas Presents

On Christmas Day, the whole family will take it in turns to draw a present from a bowl called the Urn of Fate. There is only one present each, so it is effectively a kind of lucky dip. Children have to wait until Epiphany on 6 January to hang up their stockings by the chimney and then wait for *La Befana* (The Old Woman) to fill them. The story is that the Three Wise Men came to the Befana's house asking for directions to the stable where the infant Jesus lay. She was busy and told them she couldn't help. When they asked if she could come with them, she again refused. Later, when they had gone, she regretted her decision, and set out to find them but never could. Not knowing which was the Christ child she gave every child she met a treat. It is said that naughty children only get a lump of coal!

## Italy in its spare time
### Italian TV

There is a theory that the quality of Italian TV doesn't matter to Italians because it's just part of the furniture, the *focolare domestico* (domestic hearth) as they call it. It's certainly something they love to hate. Flick through the six national channels, three government-owned (RAI Uno, RAI Due and

## Georgia

Not unlike Mariah Carey or Madonna in terms of her fame, Georgia has been a  massive star in Italy for over ten years, because of her amazing voice. You will probably also see pictures of her in Italian magazines and advertising billboards.

## Eros Ramazotti

Ramazotti is a 41-year-old singer/songwriter who is very famous in Italy. Although not that well known in Britain, he has had huge success throughout the world, selling over 30 million records!. His songs are so personalthat  his fans often feel he is a friend rather than a star and apparently often write to him with their personal problems!

## Luciano Pavarotti

The most famous opera singer in the world, Pavarotti is an Italian legend. Born in Modena in northern Italy in 1935, Pavarotti has been singing opera professionally since 1961. One of his televised perfomances in 1977 had the biggest audience ever for any opera on TV and his fame exploded further when he sang *Nessun Dorma*, the theme music to the 1990 World Cup. He is the only opera singer to have a number one album in the UK pop charts. A little known fact is that he is a huge fan of show-jumping – so much so that he set up one of the horse world's big annnual events, the Pavarotti International!

RAI Tre) and three others the property of Prime Minister Silvio Berlusconi (Italia 1, Rete 4 and Canale 5). You will most likely find yourself watching a chat show, a quiz show, or a variety show. There are over 600 local channels around Italy, which all reflect the regional areas and their interests, depending on where you are. There will, however, be many programmes that you recognize like *The Simpsons* and *South Park*, both of which are immensely popular in Italy. The difference being that they will be dubbed (where the voices are recorded over in Italian) so look out for Homer and Bart speaking fluent Italian!

### English spoken!
You might be surprised to find that the English language – of all things – is considered really cool in Italy. It's really trendy for Italians to use English words and you'll see that lots of advertising slogans are in English, too, for the same reason.

If you listen to the radio, you'll hear that some news reports are read in both Italian and English.

### Pop Music
As elsewhere in Europe, the Italian charts divide between Italian stars, usually singing in Italian, with some British and American singers and bands, not all of whom you'd expect to have an international following.

### Italian Books and Comic strips
*Lupo Alberto* has been appearing in comic strips since 1973 and just keeps getting more popular every year.

He's a pale blue wolf – not a million miles from Wile E. Coyote of *Looney Tunes* fame – who spends his time trying to get in among the chickens on the Mackenzie Farm. Mostly he's pretty hungry! You will find the comic books throughout Italy. They have been translated into loads of languages but there are no English language books at present.

Meanwhile, the *Geronimo Stilton* books are an Italian phenomenon to rival Harry Potter – in less than three years they have sold nearly 2 million copies. Stilton is a journalist who edits the *Rodent's Gazette* on the Isle of Mice. More importantly, he moonlights as an amateur detective. He is accompanied on his extraordinary investigations by his sister Thea and a motley cast of dozens. The books have now been translated into English – and 34 other languages! – but remember, you read it here first!

# A School Day in Italy

If you like sleeping late, Italian school is definitely not for you. The Italian school day usually runs from 8.30am to 1pm, six days a week, Monday to Saturday. There is no lunch break and you are mostly expected to do your homework in the afternoon. On the plus side, you don't have to wear a uniform.

The school year varies a little from region to region, but is roughly from mid-September to mid-June. As a rule of thumb, the further south you are – that is, the hotter the summer weather – the later the year starts. There are three terms (*trimestri*) and you get a little over two weeks off at Christmas and just one week at Easter. The summer holiday, though, more than makes up for the early starts. It lasts nearly three months!

Although most children have some kind of pre-school education, you don't actually have to start school until you are six, when you have to enrol at the *scuola elementare* (elementary school). You have to learn a foreign language: English is by far the most popular, although French, German and Spanish are also taught.

At the end of primary school, you have to pass an exam to gain a *Licenza Elementare* (Primary School Certificate). If you don't get this, you might get held back a year until you do pass while all your friends go on to secondary school. It's certainly one way to make sure you work hard!

There are two levels of secondary school. The lower level is the *scuola media* ('middle school'), which takes you from the age of 11 to 14. You have to earn a *Diploma di Licenza di Scuola Media* (Middle School Certificate) before you can go on to the *scuola superiore* ('higher school'), which are a bit like our sixth-form colleges.

The main difference is that these are specialist schools that set you off on your route to a career, whether it's as an engineer, architect, scientist – or whatever! Almost everyone stays on until they are 18, although only the first two years are actually compulsory.

If you've gone to a technical school, once you've passed your final exam you can officially call yourself a *perito* (expert) in your chosen area! How cool is that?

## There's nowhere else like VENICE

**Venice is where the 'high street' is a river, and your bus is a boat**

**And your taxi is a gondola**

**It's a maze of canals, arches and bridges...**

**A chessboard of sunshine and shadow**

**A treasure trove of curiosities**

**This place is perfect for playing hide-and-seek...**

**Just be careful - it's easy to get lost here!**

**At Carnival time in February, lots of the locals dress up in masks and variations of old-time costume**

Hey, it takes all sorts! Oh, and another thing – angels are everywhere

# Fabulous Buildings and Sights

**I**taly is home to some of the greatest sights in the world. This is just a selection of amazing places, some of which are world-famous, some unknown.

## Lombardy: Rock Drawings

The Valcamonica Valley takes its name from a now vanished people called the Camunni, whom the Romans defeated in 16 BC. Situated in the foothills of the Alps, the rocks of the valley wall have been worn smooth by the passing of Ice Age glaciers. Valcamonica only came to the world's attention in 1909 when it was discovered that the people of the area had been scratching figures – the locals call them *pitoti* (puppets) – into the hard rock for the last 10,000 years. These drawings are a

## ═Ten great things to see or do in Rome═

☞ **The Forum**

☞ **Trevi Fountain** The name comes from the three roads that meet there. If you throw a coin in, it's said to guarantee that you'll return to Rome one day.

☞ **The Colosseum** It could seat an extraordinary 50,000 people. Now there seem to be that many cats hanging around!

☞ **The Pantheon**

☞ **Spanish Steps** The stairs are actually French.

☞ **The Sistine Chapel**

☞ **Walk down the Via Appia** Especially on Sundays when some of it is barred to traffic.

☞ **St Peter's Basilica**

☞ **Shop on the Via Veneto**

☞ **An afternoon in the Villa Borghese** Rome's loveliest park has a small zoo, train rides, pony rides and bicycles for hire. And lots of space to picnic!

There are nearly 1,000 churches in Rome. Don't let your parents try and drag you to all of them!

---

unique record of human life and of civilization. There are hundreds of thousands of them. The earliest figures are of hunting animals, such as deer. Later, around 5,000 years ago, male and female dancers start to appear. Alongside them are domesticated animals, such as pigs and cows. What may be religious images of the sun are also from this period. About 80% of the figures in the valley actually date from the Iron Age. Warriors, riders, farming scenes, birds, houses, footprints, snakes, circles, spears – the variety is endless.

The Roman conquest of the Camunni was a watershed. Work dwindled after that. But it has never stopped. If you know where to look, you'll see some cars scratched into the rocks, too!

## Is The Tower of Pisa Meant to Lean?

Italians love the Leaning Tower of Pisa just the way it is and look upon it with pride. It is a world-famous Italian icon – on a par with the Eiffel Tower in Paris – and has always tipped to the side without ever having fallen over. The suggestion that work should be undertaken to straighten it is usually met with howls of protest. Some Italians historians have even suggested that perhaps the Tower was meant to lean. After all, you only have to visit Rome or Florence to realize that the Italians have been building works of extraordinary complexity and structural ingenuity for centuries. Is it harder to believe that such a gifted people could have got something as simple as a tower so wrong – or was their skill in architecture such that a tower that leant at an angle would seem both a technical challenge and an aesthetic delight? We don't know, to be frank. What do you think?

## Hidden Underground Rome

Everyone who comes to Rome will probably see the Sistine Chapel and the Colosseum and many other

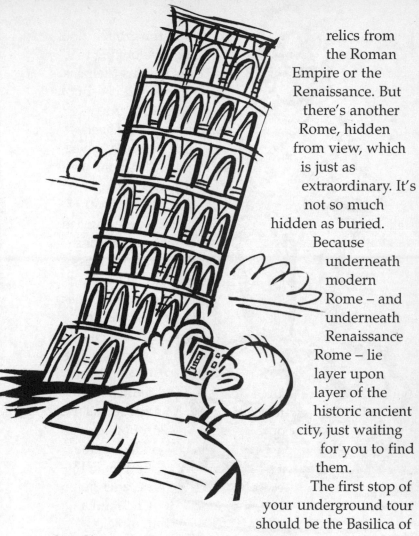

relics from the Roman Empire or the Renaissance. But there's another Rome, hidden from view, which is just as extraordinary. It's not so much hidden as buried. Because underneath modern Rome – and underneath Renaissance Rome – lie layer upon layer of the historic ancient city, just waiting for you to find them.

The first stop of your underground tour should be the Basilica of San Clemente. Deep under the basilica, you can see almost 2,000 years of history if you look through an iron grill in the floor. Beneath you are the remains of the crowded residential quarters destroyed in Nero's fire of

**Statue of Mithras**

AD 64 and the ground floor of a villa belonging to Titus Flavius Clemens, consul and cousin of the Emperor Domitian. This is pagan Rome, where the Christians were a persecuted minority and part of the house was turned into a secret meeting-place for prayer. Across the corridor, there is a temple dedicated to the Persian god Mithras, whose cult included the ritual slaying of a bull, an animal it regarded as the source of life. First evident in the Empire in the decades before Christ, this temple is probably from the cult's peak of popularity at the end of the second century AD (even the Emperor converted).

Not long after the Roman Empire was converted to

Christianity by the Emperor Constantine – who was crowned Emperor in England (actually in Yorkshire on the site of York Minster) – the first Christian church was built on this site. It became one of the most popular and beautiful in Rome. The Empress Theodora, wife of the sixth-century Byzantine Emperor Justinian the Great, liked it so much she had her portrait painted on the wall. Sadly, this church fell to the Norman, Robert Guiscard, whose men pillaged the city and burned much of it to the ground in 1084. The church's underground history lay undiscovered for 800 years, until one day in 1857 an Irish Dominican priest named Father Mullooly broke through the rubble.

There is also the Necropolis (City of the Dead) beneath St Peter's Basilica in the Vatican. St Peter the Apostle, who founded the Catholic Church, was crucified upside down at Nero's circus and buried in a nearby cemetery. The first church of St Peter – as well as its current replacement, St Peter's Basilica – was built on top of that cemetery. The altar was positioned exactly above Peter's tomb. The site wasn't excavated until 1940 when the amazed archaeologists found street after street of two-storey mausoleums, Christian symbols sitting alongside the ancient gods of Rome and Greece. There were houses and shops, too – an entire section of the old Roman city!

Directly beneath the altar, the bones of an old but strong man were found in a box hidden in the wall of an empty tomb and it is said that this is the body of St Peter. After over 20 years of forensic work, the bones were finally declared to be those of the saint.

## A Mystery in Stone

Castel del Monte was built by the Holy Roman
Emperor Frederick II on his return from the Crusades
in the 1240s. It sits on a commanding hill 549 metres
(1,800 ft) above the Puglian plain. Frederick II was an
unusual emperor. His learning was such that he was
known as 'the wonder of the age'. The dispute that
drove a wedge between the Empire and the Church
and divided Italy into Guelphs and Ghibellines started
during his reign. He was barred from the Church
twice, the second time in 1227 for failing to launch the
Sixth Crusade as he had promised. When he
subsequently did launch it the following year, the pope
was even more cross, complaining bitterly that he
wasn't ready! But the Crusade was a personal triumph
for Frederick and he was crowned King of Jerusalem.
When he died, many believed he would return from
the dead to rule for 1,000 years.

Castel del Monte is a mysterious building,
clearly designed by someone who knew a lot about
maths and thought that some numbers had magical,
mystical properties. In particular, the number eight.
The tower is octagonal; there is an octagonal-shaped
courtyard surrounded by eight towers, each of which
has two floors with eight rooms each.

For sceptics, it was just a hunting lodge with a sense
of humour. For mystics, it has secret alignments with
the stars, or was a secret meeting-place for the seekers
of the Holy Grail. Whatever it was, it wasn't a castle in
the accepted sense of the word as it has no meaningful
defences.

## The Duomo in Florence

When Florentines – the people of Florence, not the biscuit – are homesick for their city, they say they have *nostalgia del cupolone* (homesickness for the dome). Who can blame them? The proper name for the cathedral is Santa Maria del Fiore but no one calls it that. To everyone it is the Duomo.

The church itself dates back in places to the sixth or seventh century and, legend has it, stands on the site of a Roman temple to Mars, the god of war. It is the fourth largest church in the world with a dome so big and high off the ground that when the architect Filippo Brunelleschi came to build it, he had to invent a new building technique. In the past, domes had been built using immense scaffolding structures on

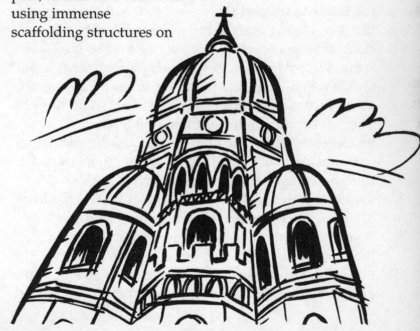

the inside to support the weight as the dome went up.
But Santa Maria was too big for that. Brunelleschi
claimed he knew a different way it could be built – but
refused to tell anyone, even his employers, what it was!

When they challenged him, he produced an egg and
asked each of them if they could make it stand upright.
They all tried and none of them could. Finally it was
Brunelleschi's turn. He took the egg and smacked it on
the table, flattening one end. Of course, it now stood
upright. Everyone else was outraged. 'That's obvious!'
they said. 'We could have done that if we'd thought of
it!' Brunelleschi replied: 'Yes, but you didn't and I did.
If you had seen my plans for the dome, you could
build that too!'.

Among Brunelleschi's many inventions was the crane.
He was so thorough in his approach that he built hooks

☞ **The Duomo**

☞ **The Baptistry** – Ghiberti's doors are among the great works of Renaissance art.

☞ **Museo del Bargello** – More statues than you can shake a stick at. Not that they encourage that sort of thing.

☞ **Ponte Vecchio** – Used to have all sorts of shops on it until 1593 when the Medici family decided the smell of the butchers was just too much and gave it to jewellers and goldsmiths instead!

☞ **Uffizi Gallery**

☞ **The Galleria dell'Accademia** – Worth it for Michelangelo's David.

☞ **The Gucci stores** – Where it all started for one of the best-known designer labels in the world.

☞ **Piazza della Signoria** – Here the famous Bonfire of the Vanities took place in 1497. Savonarola, a mad monk, persuaded half of Florence to destroy their pictures, ornaments, jewellery, fine clothes and so on to escape the wrath of God.

☞ **Boboli Gardens** – A green oasis in the city centre. And what exactly is the Medici's favourite dwarf doing to that poor tortoise? Find the statue and decide for yourself!

☞ **Sante Croce** – More great dead people than Westminster Abbey. (And prettier, to boot!)

into the brickwork to make life easier for anyone who needed to put up scaffolding around the dome later on. And the work was carried on so far above the ground and his team were taking so long to climb up and down for food and drink that he set up a wine shop and a restaurant at the top of the dome. (Though no one says what they did when they needed to go to the toilet!)

Michelangelo is buried just inside the doorway in the nearby church of Sante Croce so that, he said, when he woke again on Judgement Day the first thing he would see would be Brunelleschi's dome.

When Brunelleschi himself died, he was buried in the Duomo – the only Florentine to receive such an honour – but his tomb was so modest that it wasn't found until 1974!

## Houses carved out of Rock

In the Basilicata region of Italy – for centuries the poorest in the country – you will find the Sassi di Matera. These are houses carved out of the soft stone of the rolling hillside outside the town of Matera. No one is really sure how old they are, although there are over 100 churches or religious cells scooped out of the rock, some of which date to the eighth century. It seems more than likely, though, that people have been living in these dwellings since prehistoric times, which is a strange feeling to have when you walk around, trying to imagine what it would be like to live in one.

But if you think living in a cave would be cool – a cross between the Flintstones and the Batcave, maybe – then think again. No water, no electricity, no toilets, nothing! Really no fun at all. People only lived here if they had nowhere else to go. And they did so until quite recently. The site's strange beauty and uniqueness has now been recognized, since it was placed on the United Nations list of World Heritage Sites in 1983.

## Venice – the city of water

Venice  is one of the most famous Italian cities and is like no other city you will ever see. It is often called La Serenissima, which means 'the most serene'. One 20th century American wrote back home to his wife: 'Help! The streets are full of water!' – and he had a point! The famous Romantic poet Lord Byron, who lived in Venice, described it

☞ **The Grand Canal** – A vaporetto – or river-bus ride – down this is the best introduction to Venice. Just don't go swimming in it – it's far too dirty!

☞ **Basilica di San Marco** – Look for the originals of the bronze horses that adorn the façade. They once stood on Trajan's Arch in Rome before the Emperor Constantine took them for his Hippodrome in Byzantium. The Venetians stole them during the 4$^{th}$ crusade. Sadly, they're in the museum now.

☞ **Doge's Palace** – Remember, count those lions!

☞ **Ca'Rezzonico** – An 18$^{th}$-century museum. Look out for the carvings of slaves in chains for a reminder of the dark side of European trade.

☞ **Try and figure out the house numbers!** – Buildings here are numbered according to which quarter of the city they are in, not which street. Almost no one understands the system!

☞ **Ride in a gondola** – A 1532 law forbade excessive decoration – which is why to this day all gondolas are black!

☞ **Shop in the markets on the Rialto**

☞ **Murano** – See the world-famous glassblowers at work.

☞ **San Giorgio Maggiore** – Fantastic view of the city from the campanile (tower).

☞ **The lido** – Too much art and culture? Come here to lie on the sand and relax.

as 'the greenest island of my imagination'.

Why did anyone decide to build a city in a lagoon? No one really knows. Venice's origins are lost in the mists of time. One myth is that Venice was founded at noon on March 25 in the year 421. (In the old calendar, March 25 was New Year's Day.)

Venetians have particular reason to be thankful to alert kids. When the Doge's palace burned down in 1479, the only record of inscriptions on the wall by the great Renaissance poet Petrarch were in the notebook of Marin Sanudo. He was eight at the time. You never know when these things will come in useful! (Marin went on to write a history of the world in 55 – count them – volumes.)

## Walking on water

It's great to ride in a gondola or river bus down the Grand Canal. But you might be surprised to learn that

the best way to really explore Venice is on foot.

Venice is packed full of extraordinary art and architecture. But the greatest work of art here is the city itself with endless passages and alleyways that open up into large squares.

Venice is also sinking – very, very slowly. It has gone down by more than 20cm since 1990! But the Italian government – and campaign charities like Venice in Peril – are doing everything they can to lessen the erosion of this amazing city.

### Venetian animals

Lions are one of the symbols of the city and they are everywhere. Carvings of them, anyway. At least 75 have been counted on the Porta della Carta – one of the doors of the Doge's Palace – alone!

There are plenty of real animals, too. You will find lots of cats and many birds. The armies of pigeons in St Mark's Square are just as famous as those in Trafalgar Square – but the city also gets plenty of visits from seagulls, who are driven in by storms out at sea, and swallows who arrive en masse in summer to gorge on mosquitos. In medieval Venice, there used to be lots of horses and mules. So many, in fact, that a 14$^{th}$ century law compelled them to wear bells. But the Venetian discovery of the art of

---

### Facts about Venice

- ☞ There are over 150 canals in Venice, totalling about 28 miles in length. Across these lie about 400 bridges.
- ☞ The main thoroughfare, the Grand Canal, which was once a river, twists through the city in a back-to-front S-shape.
- ☞ The Grand Canal is two miles long and between 40 and 76 yards wide. On average, it is 9 feet deep.
- ☞ The other canals are typically only around 12 feet across and a few feet deep.
- ☞ The city itself is built on 117 islands and islets in the lagoon.

---

making arched bridges changed all that and made water the best way of getting about.

## Siena Cathedral

One of the many striking things about the cathedral in Siena is its inlaid marble pavement with portraits of church fathers, biblical scenes and many other – sometimes obscure – symbols (among them snakes and newts). The floor took 40 artists over 200 years to complete.

Pride of place as you enter from the west is the portrait of Hermes Trismegistus (try saying that quickly), one of the great figures of Renaissance thought. His works were regarded as a combination of Christian and Greek traditions with an added layer of cosmic belief. He was very influential, particularly for those who saw what we would now call science as a means of unlocking the divine secrets of God. One such secret, which people thought he could help unravel, was alchemy – turning base metal into gold and refining the elixir of life, a potion that made you immortal. Unfortunately for would-be alchemists – and, indeed, for whoever commissioned the portrait for the floor of the cathedral – Trismegistus was revealed to be a fake in the early 17th century.

## Greek Drama in Syracuse

The *Teatro Greco* (Greek Theatre) looking out across the city to the sea in Syracuse, Sicily, was carved out of the local white rock in the fifth century BC. One of the largest classical theatres in the world, it could seat 15,000 people. The first performance of the great Greek playwright Aeschylus' *The Persians* was staged here. And Aeschylus himself was here to witness it.

## Trulli, Madly, Deeply

The history of Italy has spanned more than 3,000 years of peoples, foods and cultures that have influenced the country as a whole. It is therefore unusual to come across a building style that is only used in one region, as is the case with the *trulli* of Puglia in the area around Alberobello. The houses here are unlike house anywhere else in Italy or Europe. They have a conical, loose stone roof that looks a bit like an upturned beehive. The roofs also have strange symbols on them and the walls are almost always painted white.

There are many theories about how these houses

## Ten great things to see or do elsewhere

☞ **Naples** – The best pizza in the world.

☞ **Siena** – Run around in the vast cloak-shaped Piazza del Campo. Climb the tower for astonishing views.

☞ **Pompeii/Herculaneum** – Imagine what life in a Roman city was really like.

☞ **Pisa** – Not seeing the Leaning Tower would be a crime.

☞ **San Gimignano** – Tuscany's loveliest village.

☞ **Etna** – Fancy climbing a volcano?

☞ **The Amalfi coast** – You won't see a more breath-takingly beautiful coastline anywhere in Europe.

☞ **Ravenna** – The best Byzantine mosaics outside of Byzantium (or Istanbul, as it is called today).

☞ **Piedmont and Lombardy** – Eat some truffle. You decide if it's worth the money! (But make sure it's your parent's money.)

☞ **Gargano peninsula** – Right at the heel of Italy, this boasts some of the best beaches in Italy set in one of its most stunning national parks.

came about. One suggestion is that they were built in this way so that they could be easily dismantled by their owners if they wanted to move!

# Great Inventors, Famous Artists and Scientists

## Archimedes

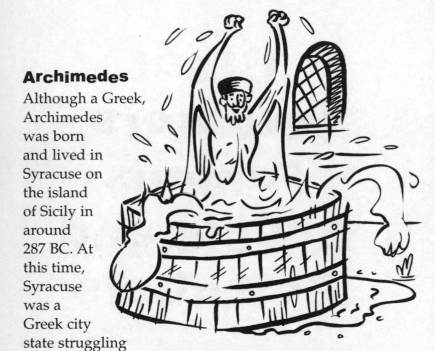

Although a Greek,
Archimedes
was born
and lived in
Syracuse on
the island
of Sicily in
around
287 BC. At
this time,
Syracuse
was a
Greek city
state struggling
to keep its independence from the power struggle
between Rome and Carthage in the Punic Wars.
Considered the greatest mathematician until Isaac
Newton, 1800 years later, Archimedes is best known
for leaping out of his bath and running naked down
the street shouting *'Eureka!'* (Greek for 'I have found
it!'). He was also active on behalf of Syracuse against
the Romans and built a weapon to defend his

hometown with called The Claw, which terrified the enemy because it was capable of lifting a fully manned ship out of the water at the pull of a rope. Archimedes was slain by a Roman soldier when the city finally fell in 212 BC. He was lost in thought tracing a design in the dust on the courtyard floor when the soldier burst into his house and demanded his name. Archimedes only said,'I beg you, do not disturb this,' and the soldier stabbed him for his insolence.

## Bartolomeo Cristofori

Born in Padua in 1655, Bartolomeo Cristofori was the man who invented the piano. Cristofori called his new invention a *gravicembalo col piano e forte* (a harpsichord that plays soft and loud). Not very catchy, is it? Which is possibly why it wasn't until his creation got its current name that it reached a wider audience and its qualities properly recognised.

## Dante Alighieri

Born in Florence in 1265, Dante is still considered one of the greatest writers in the world. He spent much of his early career involved in the complex plots and counterplots of the Guelph/Ghibelline war (see Italian History on page 24). When both he and his sons were exiled from Florence to Ravenna, Dante wrote *La Divina Commedia* (The Divine Comedy), one of the greatest works of world literature, from which the modern-day Italian language is said to have been born.

He died in 1321 and is buried in the church of San Francesco in Ravenna.

In Florence, you can go and sit on the bench in the Piazza del Duomo where Dante used to sit and watch the great cathedral being built. (It's known as Dante's seat.) You can also see the monument the Florentines erected to his memory after his death. It is in the Santa Croce, near the tombs of great Italians such as Michelangelo and Galileo.

## Enzo Ferrari

Born in Modena in 1898, Ferrari became obsessed with racing cars at the age of 10, when his father took him to see a race at the track in Bologna. After fighting in the First World War, Enzo found a job with Alfa-Romeo, where he began racing cars professionally in 1919, quickly becoming one of Italy's leading drivers.

In 1923 he raced at the circuit of Sivocci at Ravenna. Watching in the crowd was the father of one of Italy's war heroes, the flying ace, Francesco Baracca. He was so impressed by the courage and determination with which Ferrari competed that he presented the young driver with his son's squadron badge. It was a prancing horse on a yellow shield. Ferrari would make the badge his own: it appears on his cars to this day.

If you want to see Ferrari cars through all the different stages, there is a fantastic place in Italy called the Galleria Ferrari museum, at Maranello, outside Modena in northern Italy.

## Galileo

One of the great scientists of all time, Galileo has been called the father of modern physics, modern astronomy *and* science. Born in 1564, he was a pioneer of the type of experimental science that required proof of its theories through controlled experiments. The story of Galileo dropping balls of different weights from the Leaning Tower of Pisa to test if they would fall at the same speed is typical of his approach. As an astronomer, Galileo was the first European to observe sunspots and the first person to identify the mountains on the Moon. His successful inventions include the microscope and the thermometer. Among his less successful ideas was a comb that doubled as an eating utensil – yuck! – and something that looked

### Alfa-Romeo

It is said that Henry Ford, the inventor of the Ford motor car, was so in awe of Alfa-Romeos that he would doff his hat whenever he saw one pass. Dating from 1910, the company has won more Grand Prix than any other car. Enzo Ferrari wept the first time he beat them.

If you want to know more about Alfa-Romeo, you can visit the Alfa-Romeo Museum, in Arese, near Milan.

### Bugatti

Believe it or not, these legendary racing cars began their life in 1898 as a motor tricycle – built by 17-year-old engineering genius Ettore Bugatti for the Paris to Bordeaux race. It was placed first and Bugatti had found himself a career.

Bugatti's most extraordinary car was the Type 41 Royale, also known as the Golden Bugatti, launched in 1929. Designed for the super-wealthy – specifically for royalty, as the name suggests – only six of these cars were ever made. They were over 22 feet long and stood over five feet high – even at the bonnet! The engine was originally designed to fit into an aeroplane, but when Bugatti lost that contract, he decided to put the engine into a car instead. Although the car itself was a commercial disaster, the engines were not. The Italian government bought hundreds of them to power trains.

The Royale is still the largest car ever to go into production. The engine is still the largest ever fitted in a commercially available car. And the Royale is also the world's most expensive car – one changed hands for $15m in 1990.

Alfa-Romeos may have won more Grand Prix, but Bugattis have won more races, despite ceasing production in 1947.

## Lamborghini

Ferruccio Lamborghini actually made his fortune designing tractors. But one day he happened to meet Enzo Ferrari and complain about the engine in the Ferrari he owned. When Enzo dismissed his complaint out of hand, saying something insulting about farm mechanics, Lamborghini was so incensed he vowed revenge. He took all his money and set up a car factory just down the road from Ferrari's.

But Lamborghini was a much better engineer than he was a racing driver. The first time he raced one of his cars he ended up driving it through the front of a café. He cheekily stayed to order some red wine!

There are two Lamborghini museums you can visit. One is attached to the firm's factory in Sant'Agata Bolognese near Bologna. The other, which houses examples of pretty much everything Ferrucio did in a purpose-built building, is in Dosso, just down the road. Both are free, but by appointment only.

remarkably like a ballpoint pen. In 1633, Galileo was tried before the Spanish Inquisition for heresy because he believed that Earth revolved around the sun – contrary to the teachings of the Roman Catholic Church. Although Galileo escaped with his life by begging for mercy and denouncing his own work, he spent the rest of his days under house arrest, eventually dying in 1642. It's a bit creepy, but you can see the middle finger of Galileo's right hand in the Museo di Storia della Scienza in Florence!

## Giuseppe Garibaldi

One of Italy's modern heroes – and one of the great revolutionary heroes of the 19th century – Garibaldi did more than almost anyone to free Italy from Austrian rule. He has been called the Nelson Mandela of his day. Born in Nice (when it was still Italian) in 1807, he led two attempted uprisings, in 1834 and 1848, before finally succeeding in 1860. He died peacefully at Caprera in 1882.

## Giotto

Giotto was born in 1267 and is credited as the first Western artist to make you believe the emotions of the people he painted. It is said that the pope was scouring Italy for its greatest artists and sent his courtiers into Florence to gather some sample drawings. Most artists, delighted at the thought of a possible commission from the pope himself, produced fantastically complex sketches for the courtier. Giotto simply drew a perfect circle on a single piece of paper – the catch being that he had done it freehand! If you're very clever, you could do this, too, but it is almost impossible for most humans. Try it! (The pope was suitably impressed, by the way.)

You can visit the Cappella degli Scrovegni in Padua, where Giotto spent four years frescoing scenes from

the New Testament – an achievement on the same scale as the Sistine Chapel. He died in 1337.

## Leonardo da Vinci

Everyone knows that Leonardo, born in 1452, was a genius. Not only did he paint the *Mona Lisa* and *The Last Supper*, he conducted experiments in anatomy and invented the helicopter, submarine and tank. Less well-known are his invention of the cluster bomb, a robot and a calculator. He also experimented with solar power. Leonardo didn't get everything right, however – he believed that the moon reflected the sun's light because its surface was covered with water and his inventiveness almost destroyed his painting of *The Last Supper*. Not content to use the traditional fresco technique of painting on fresh plaster, Leonardo's paint started flaking almost as soon as he had finished the picture. It has been the subject of endless restoration since the seventeenth century, most recently during an 18-year-stretch that ended only in 1995. *The Last Supper* is in the convent of Santa Maria delle Grazie in Milan. It is said the face of Judas is that of the prior of the convent, whom Leonardo disliked. He died in 1519.

## Michelangelo Buonarroti

Born in 1475, Michelangelo first trained as a sculptor. Even if he had never painted, works like his famous statue of David (now in the Galleria dell'Accademia in Florence) would have ensured his immortality. He was 24 when he made David, and he did so, to everyone's astonishment, from a flawed block of marble. His other great work – some would say the greatest work of art in the world – is the ceiling of the Sistine Chapel in the Vatican in Rome, which took four years to complete (and eight years to restore in the 1990s). When Michelangelo was painting *The Last Judgement* panel of the Sistine Chapel, the pope's master of ceremonies

nagged him incessantly for a glimpse of the great work. When at last it was unveiled, the poor man was horrified to see himself depicted in Hell. He stormed off to see the pope and begged him to intervene. But he got no joy. 'God has given me authority in Heaven and on Earth,' the pope responded. 'But my writ does not extend to Hell.' Michelangelo died in 1564.

## Marco Polo

The greatest explorer of his day, Marco Polo was born into a prosperous merchant's family on the Adriatic in 1254. In 1271, he set out with his father on the Silk Road – the great trading route into and out of the East – one of the first Europeans to do so. They made it all the way to the court of Kubla Khan in China, where

Polo's talents were soon recognized and he was rewarded with the governorship of one of Khan's provinces. Father and son returned to Venice in 1295.

The story goes that neither was recognized by their family until they threw back their filthy clothes and slit open the linings to allow a flood of emeralds, rubies and pearls to escape. The Venetians nicknamed Marco Polo *Milion* because everything he talked about on his travels was always in 'millions'. (It's also the original title of his book of travels.) On his deathbed, his last words were, 'I only told the half of what I saw'. Some people doubt he ever travelled as far as he did. Scholars have wondered why he never spoke about the use of chopsticks or the existence of the Great Wall given the time he spent in China, for instance. On the other hand, he was the first European to note the existence of Japan. No one knows for sure. What do you think?

A part of his house still stands in Venice, tucked

away behind the church of San Giovanni Crisostomo. The area is called the *Corta Seconda del Milion*. Marco Polo must have walked there countless times. But perhaps not millions! He died in 1324.

## Antonio Meucci

Born in 1808, this was the man who actually invented the telephone. He did so in 1849 and began to patent it in 1871. Poverty and ill health meant that when he thought his idea had been stolen from him by Alexander Graham Bell, he was never in a position to defend himself properly. Sadly, he died, old and broke, in 1896.

## Alessandro Della Spina

A Dominican friar from Pisa, Della Spina is credited with the revolutionary invention of spectacles. When he died in 1317, he had an inscription placed on his tomb saying so – but then the tomb of his

friend, Salvino degli Armati, says the same thing! His invention is generally dated to around 1285. What is definite is that spectacles were commonplace by 1352. We know this because there is a fresco on the wall of the Gothic church of San Nicolò in Treviso, which dates from that year and includes a number of portraits of Dominican monks wearing reading glasses!

## Giuseppe Verdi

Over a century after his death, Verdi is still one of the most popular Italian composers of all time. Born in 1813 when Italy was ruled by Napoleon, his career coincided with the rise of Italian nationalism – the Risorgimento – and the eventual creation of an independent Italian state. From the 1840s onwards, Verdi had huge success with operas like *Il Trovatore*, *La Traviata*, *Aida* and *Rigoletto*.

Bizarrely, Verdi's own name proved to be an acronym of *Vittorio Emanuele Re D'Italia* (Victor Emmanuel King of Italy) – one of the leading figures in the Italian Nationalist Movement. Partisans plotting on the king's behalf started using Verdi's name (apparently with Verdi's support) as a code. When Verdi died in 1901, some 250,000 mourners attended his funeral.

# Food and Drink

**E**ven if you don't know anything about Italy, you will know something about its world-famous food. Even if you've never eaten a pizza, you will surely have seen one. There can't be many who have never eaten pasta, whether spaghetti, ravioli, lasagne or another of its dozens of variations. Italian ice cream, too, is found all over the world.

Contrary to what the French might think, it was Italy that first developed the culinary arts during the Renaissance. The first printed cookery book was written by an Italian called Bartolomeo Platina in 1475. His *De Honesta Voluptate* was an immediate success, going through 30 editions in its first 100 years and being translated into many different languages, although English wasn't one of them. We had to wait until 1967 when it appeared (bizarrely) as a Christmas gift from the Mallinckrodt Chemical Corporation of St Louis to its customers!

Pizza and pasta are so widely available that this tends to blind us to the variety of other food on offer in Italy. Every region is different. In northern Italy, for  instance, dishes tend to be cooked with butter rather than olive oil (as they are in the south), or lard, as they often prepared in central Italy. Rice dishes like risotto are more popular in the north than in the south, especially in Lombardy, where polenta – a kind of grain – is also widely used. Venetian food, as you might expect, contains a great deal of fish and seafood. There are 63 different kinds of fish or seafood on the menu in Venice, some of which, like *moleche*, a tiny soft-shelled crab, you won't find anywhere else in Italy. Sicilian cooking, which often includes ingredients like raisins and almonds in its savoury dishes, still reflects an Arabic influence dating from the Arab control of the island between the ninth and eleventh centuries.

## The Day in Food

As in Spain and Portugal, *colazione* (breakfast) in Italy generally involves little more than a coffee and a sweet

┌─────────────────────────────────────────────────┐
│ **A typical lunch menu**
│
│ ☞ **Antipasti** (starters)
│ A proper lunch would begin at 1pm with antipasti, a
│ range of starters that would usually include a selection of
│ cold meats, vegetables dishes, seafood and other
│ delights. (Some restaurants will let you spend the entire
│ meal eating antipasti.)
│
│ ☞ **Il primo** (first course)
│ This might well be pasta or risotto, but could also be
│ soup.
│
│ ☞ **Il secondo** (second course)
│ This is the central dish of the meal, being a meat or fish
│ dish probably served on its own.
│
│ ☞ **Contorni** (side dishes)
│ These are served separately and can be anything from
│ salads, to vegetables in amazing sauces.
│
│ ☞ **Il dolce** (dessert)
│ Italians have amazing puddings ranging from ice cream
│ to traditional desserts from the region.
└─────────────────────────────────────────────────┘

pastry or croissant. *Pranzo* (lunch) is the main meal of the day. The pressure of the modern world has meant that huge lunches followed by an afternoon nap are rapidly becoming a thing of the past. Nevertheless, you will still come across plenty of shops that shut for a couple of hours at lunchtime, as do all banks.

*La cena* (supper) is similar to lunch and tends to be later than you might be used to at around 8pm. It is traditional for families to eat together.

## Something to make you think twice!

Traditionally, dried pasta was made from dough which was kneaded by foot! Men and women would tread on it – sometimes for a whole day – to make it flexible enough to use.

Some of the earliest recipes for pasta dishes suggest that it should be topped with things like sugar and cinnamon!

To find out more about the phenomenon that is pasta, visit the Museo Nazionale delle Paste Alimentari (The National Museum of Pasta) in Rome.

## The Marco Polo Myth

It's often said that Marco Polo introduced pasta to Italy when he returned from China in 1295. This is

Think you know about pasta? How many kinds of pasta can you name? Write them down and see how you got on compared to this list:

| | | |
|---|---|---|
| Agnolini | Fusilli | Ravioli |
| Agnolotti | Lasagna | Ricce |
| Anellini | Lingue di | Rigatoni |
| Bavette | passero | Ruote |
| Bigoli | Lumache | Sedani |
| Bombolotti | Lumaconi | Spaghetti |
| Bucatini | Maccheroni alla | Strozzapreti |
| Cannelloni | chitarra | Tagliatelle |
| Capelli d'angelo | Maltagliati | Tortellini |
| Cappelletti | Millerighe | Tortiglioni |
| Conchiglie | Orecchiette | Trenette |
| Farfalle | Pappardelle | Vermicelli |
| Fettuccine | Penne | Ziti |

Some kinds of pasta have weird and wonderful names. Which of these are genuine, do you think?

1. Sparrows' tongues
2. Small worms
3. Angel hair
4. Little ears
5. Little strings
6. Slugs

Surprisingly, the answer is all of them! *Lingue di passero* (1); *vermicelli* (2); *capelli d'angelo* (3); *orecchiette* (4); *spaghetti* (5); *lumaconi* (6). So just be careful what you ask for in restaurants!

completely untrue. The first reference to something like modern pasta is to a *bariscella piena de macaronis* (a basket full of – presumably dried – macaroni) in the will of a Genoese merchant in 1279. But there is also evidence of food very like pasta dating back to Greek times and a fourth-century BC Etruscan relief from Caere, or modern-day Cerveteri, about 80 km (50 miles) north of Rome, shows a set of tools that look exactly like pasta-making equipment! No one knows how to read the Etruscan language, though, so we can't be sure.

There is some confusion about where the Marco Polo myth began, too, and competing explanations may be myths themselves. One traces it back to an ad for a Canadian soup company in the 1920s. Another says that the story first appeared in 1929 in an American magazine called *Macaroni Journal*, published by the American Association of Pastas. According to this source, one of Marco Polo's sailors was captivated by the sight of a Chinese girl preparing noodles. The sailor's name? Spaghetti, of course!

## Pizza

Although not as ancient as pasta, pizzas go back a long way. The first known reference to pizza is AD 997, although it seems more than likely that pizza and Greek pitta bread share the same distant origin. Some versions of pizza in Italy, known as *pizza bianca* (white pizza), are actually very close to pitta bread and don't have toppings. They tend to be found in the northern regions,

such as Tuscany and Liguria. The true home of pizza as
we know it today is Naples. As elsewhere in Italy, the
pizza base here is always thin. The very idea of 'deep
pan' or – worse – a pizza crust filled with tasteless
cheese would fill most Italians with horror. The ideal
Neapolitan pizza should be baked in a wood-fired brick
oven heated to a terrifying 400°C (752°F). The *marinara*
pizza has oil, tomato, garlic, oregano and gets its name
from Naples' sailors, who are known as the *marinari*.
The pizza *margherita* celebrates the visit to Naples by an
Italian queen of that name towards the end of the
nineteenth century. The tomato, basil and mozzarella are
meant to recall the colours of the then new Italian flag.

## Hunting for Truffles

What are truffles exactly? We're not talking chocolate here. We're talking about a rare form of mushroom that grows underground at the base of trees. They are considered a delicacy throughout the world. The biggest can be the size of a football.

Whatever their size, truffles are invisible on the surface and you need animals with an acute sense of smell to sniff them out, which is where the dogs and the pigs come in... You could say that truffles taste unlike anything else – and once you've tasted one, you won't ever forget it. The white truffle season is from November to February; the *Fiera del Tartufo Bianco* (White Truffle Fair) in Alba runs on four successive weekends through to mid-November.

The defining mark of a big truffle area is the ritual of the truffle hunt, which tends to be confined to areas like Umbria and Piedmont. Imagine being woken up in the dead of night to go creeping silently through the

Truffles are a greatly prized delicacy: the largest white truffle ever recorded – more valuable than the black – weighed more than 2 kg (4 lbs). Found near Alba in the Piedmont in 1951, it was sold for the equivalent of over £3,000 in today's money. Truffles of any size are highly lucrative. Pound for pound, only saffron is more expensive among foodstuffs (and saffron is dearer than gold). At current prices, 100g (2.26 lbs) of white truffle is worth about £100 or $200.

cold winter woods. You can't make a noise because you don't want to alert other truffle-hunters to where the best hunting grounds are. You might even have a pig to track down what you are looking for! Pigs are actually better at sniffing out truffles than dogs, but might be less keen to let go of the prize once they have snuffled it from the ground.

## Ice Cream

Ice desserts of any kind, whether ice cream or water ices, don't seem to have been around before the seventeenth century. Since as far back as the fourth century AD, people have known that adding salt to ice not only causes it to melt, but also brings down its temperature, creating a slushy liquid that is colder than frozen water. In the early 1600s someone realized that if you did this, and then placed a container with another liquid inside the slush, you could artificially freeze that liquid. This process is known as the endothermic effect.

Among the first such creations were the *granitas* of Sicily, icy drinks made with sugar, water and a range of flavourings – from fruit juices and rose petals to coffee. No one knows who first thought of adding in cream, but the idea was clearly in wide circulation by 1672, when 'one plate of ice cream' was on the menu at the St George's Day feast in Windsor! The first ice cream cone came centuries later, was patented in America by an Italian immigrant called Italo Marchiony on 13 December 1903 and made famous at the St Louis Fair the following year.

## Parmesan cheese

The Italian name for this is Parmigiano Reggiano and it comes from the region around Parma. It is extremely old – dating back several centuries. The great medieval Italian writer Boccaccio had a story in his *Decameron* about a land which had a mountain of Parmesan cheese in the middle of it. The people who lived there did nothing but make ravioli all day. And who can blame them?

## Parma Ham

The very best Parma ham, a very thinly cut traditional Italian ham, comes from Langhirano just outside Parma. You might be surprised to find out that Parma ham is, in fact, raw. It is salted with sea salt for a month and then dried for anything up to two years. It is an Italian speciality: by law, no other ham can call itself Parma ham.

## Some classic Italian dishes

☞ *La Caprese* – A salad from Capri with tomatoes, Mozzarella cheese and basil. A very popular *antipasto* (starter).

☞ *Crostini di Mozzarella e Alici* – Actually, *crostini*, which are slices of toasted *ciabatta* bread, come with all sorts of different toppings. *Alici* are anchovies – and if you don't leave Italy with a love of this little fish, shame on you!

☞ *Fave con Pecorino e Prosciutto* – In parts of Italy such as Tuscany, beans are far more common than

pasta. This is another classic traditional *antipasto* with the grated Pecorino cheese and chunks of strong prosciutto ham.

☞ *La Stracciatella* – A delicious egg and cheese soup from Rome with a lot of lemon in it. The cheese is Parmesan, of course!

☞ *Risotto all Milanese* – Northern Italy uses rice in its cooking a lot. Made with saffron – and the yellower the better! – the rice is cooked with beef marrow and topped with Parmesan.

☞ *Gnocchi di Patate al Sugo di Pomodoro* – Another non-pasta staple! Gnocchi are essentially balls of mashed potato which are then boiled. It's easy to turn them into rocks but they should be lovely and light and soft!

☞ *Carpa all'Ebraica* – A dish that shows the influence of Arabic cooking on Italy. This is carp with almonds and sultanas. Carp is a very meaty fish so this dish is full of flavour!

☞ *Saltimbocca* – Escalopes of veal with prosciutto and mozzarella. Absolutely delicious – although a lot of people don't like the idea of eating veal.

☞ *Piccioni di Montecarlo* – Roasted pigeons with sausage and bacon and sage. The recipe is about 800 years old. If you're feeling adventurous, you will also find rabbit, hare and wild boar on some Italian menus!

☞ *Zabaglione* – Fights it out with Tiramisu as the classic Italian pudding. It's made from eggs, sugar and a kind of sweet wine called Marsala. You might find the last a bit strong, but at least try a spoonful!

## Drinks

It's common for Italian children to start drinking a little amount of wine at family meals from a very early age – although it is always watered down first. *Spremute*, freshly squeezed fruit juices, are widely available in Italy, as are most of the soft drinks you are used to at home. For a change, you could try *Chinotto*, the Italian cola.

Tea is not widely drunk in Italy. Coffee, on the other hand, is practically the national drink. Italians were, of course, the first Europeans to drink it. No one knows quite when it was first drunk, but it probably first surfaced in Venice around the end of the 16th century. The first Italian coffee house opened in 1645 (seven years before the first English one!).

It's no surprise that most ways of describing types of coffee are Italian terms like espresso and cappuccino. The espresso machine was invented in 1946 by an Italian named Achilles Gaggia. (You'll have seen his name everywhere – they are still the Rolls-Royce of espresso makers.) The name cappuccino comes from the resemblance of the drink to the robes of the Capuchin order of monks, which have white hoods!

# Festivals and National Celebrations

It is almost impossible to count the number of festivals in Italy. There are just too many! Apart from the big national celebrations, every town will have its own local festivals involving the patron saint of the town or region. There are also countless fairs and festivities focusing around food and drink. Piedmont alone has over 30 of these, ranging from one in Cuneo dedicated to *Sua Maestà Il Salame* (His Majesty the Salami) to another in Vercelli called *Sagra della Rana*, which celebrates the many uses and virtues of frog meat – yuck! It's the first weekend in September if you're really keen. Frogs are available fried, stewed or cooked in a wide range of sauces, so if you have a hidden passion for eating frogs, this one is for you.

In general, though, the Italians are a flamboyant and fun-loving nation who take their traditional celebrations very seriously.

### *Sagra del Mandorlo in Fiore* (Festival of the Almond Blossoms)

This festival, which takes place in the first two weeks of February, was started in the 1930s as a celebration of spring in the ancient Greek city of Agrigento in Sicily, marking the time of year when the almond trees were in blossom. It has slowly mushroomed into a major international folk music and dance festival. Even if such things aren't exactly to your taste – and let's face it, they're not everyone's – what really makes the event special is its location in front of the Tempio della Concordia, probably the best-preserved Greek temple outside of Greece, and with few rivals even there. The sight of this, and the two other temples in the Valle dei Tempi, in a sea of white almond blossom, is just spectacular.

### *Festa del Cioccolato* (Feast of Chocolate)

During a three-week period each March, Turin and the surrounding region gives itself over to a celebration of the world's favourite food – chocolate. Emanuele Filiberto, Duke of Savoy, introduced chocolate to Italy in 1559, having first encountered it at the court of Charles V in Spain, in whose army he served. The Duke's court was in Turin.

### *Carnevale* (Carnival)

True carnivals developed from the rituals of the
Catholic Church during the Middle Ages and represent
a period of excess before the sacrifices of Lent. Lent is
the 40 days from Ash Wednesday until Easter Sunday
when Christians fast (or nowadays just give up
chocolate) as a way of commemorating Christ's own
40-day fast in the wilderness. (The Mardi Gras in Rio
de Janeiro is a similar celebration.)

The world's most famous carnival is in Venice.
Opinions vary as to when it started, but it may have
been as early as 1094. That's some party! For centuries
it had a reputation for wildness that was unrivalled.
Most people who came wore a costume called a *bautta*,
which seems to have been designed to give away as
few clues as possible about your identity. Secrecy was

key. You wore a black silk hood, a lace cape, a cloak called a *tabarro*, a three-cornered hat, and a white mask to cover your face – even your husband or wife wouldn't recognize you! All social differences – and most morals – were forgotten. Even Lord Byron – mad, bad, dangerous to know, and a man who loved a good time – was exhausted by it. He lived in Venice between 1817 and 1819 and complained that the carnival had turned him into an invalid at the age of 29.

Carnival in Venice is still very exciting today. How could anything not be that includes masked balls by candlelight in eighteenth-century *palazzos* on the Grand Canal?

These days, though, there are other carnivals in Italy to rival it. The one in Viareggio on the Tuscan coast, for instance, is increasingly popular – not least because of its fabulous setting. Parades of vast, colourful carnival floats make their way down graceful late nineteenth-

century avenues between the sea and the Apuan Alps.

But even this is not a patch on the carnival in Ivrea, Piedmont, now coming up to its 200th birthday. Here the Catholic year has somehow become tangled with another celebration, since the most memorable aspect of the carnival in Ivrea commemorates the local uprising against a feudal lord in 1194. The event is re-enacted in a pitched battle using oranges!

The tyrant's men stand on horse-drawn trucks, perhaps a dozen of them on each. The townspeople have a range of costumes to choose from: *diavoli* (devils), *morte* (death), *picche* (spades), *scacchi* (chess) and *pantere* (panthers). All the costumes have deep V-necked fronts for storing the oranges they are going to throw.

However, the reality is that with thousands of oranges flying through the air, it doesn't really matter what you are wearing or which side you started out on. This is especially true if you fail to wear a red hat, which for some reason signifies the town's freedom.

## Settimana Santa (Holy Week)
As part of the Holy Week, the pope leads a candle-lit procession from the Colosseum, where evening mass is held, up the Palatine Hill.

## Scoppio del Carro (Explosion of the Cart)
A cartful of fireworks is drawn through the streets of Florence on Easter Saturday by oxen and then ignited

in the Piazza del Duomo by a mechanical dove sent from the altar during mass.

### Festa del Grillo (Festival of the Cricket)

Parco delle Cascine, Florence's largest park, plays host to this annual Ascension Day ritual in which people buy caged crickets for each other!

### La Sensa (Marriage of the Sea)

This festival takes place on the first Sunday after Ascension Day. It dates back to 997, when the Doge of Venice, Pietro Orseolo, gave thanks for a Venetian victory over Croatian pirates in the Adriatic. He sailed out towards the open sea and prayed to the turbulent waters: 'Grant, O Lord, that for us and for all who sail thereon, the sea may ever be calm and quiet'. As anyone who has ever been to sea in a small boat will know, that's a lot to ask of anyone, even God.

As the centuries passed, though, the service became increasingly confident. In later years, the Doge would cast gold rings into the water, saying, 'We wed thee, O sea, in sign of our true and perpetual dominion'. Venice revived the practice in 1988. The role of the Doge is played by the city's mayor. *Doge*, by the way, was the title given to Venice's ruler.

## Festa di San Nicola (Feast of St Nicholas)

On the first Sunday in May, a procession of boats from the Apulian town of Bari follows a statue of St Nicholas out to sea to give thanks to the sailors who gave their lives to protect the saint's body from a raiding party that wanted to steal it. If that sounds like a peculiar thing for anyone to want to steal, it's worth knowing that Bari had stolen it from its rightful Byzantine-Greek keepers in 1087. (Should you ever need the information, you now know where the original Father Christmas is buried!)

## Processione dei Serpari (Procession of the Snakes)

In pagan times, the people of what is now Marsica in Abruzzo worshipped a snake goddess called Angizia, who cast a long shadow. In Cocullo each year on the first Thursday in May, a statue of St Domenico is placed on a float and carried through the town. The statue, float and everyone around is swathed in a mass of living, writhing snakes!

## La Cavalcata Sarda
(Sardinian Cavalcade)

The people of Sardinia come together in their thousands in Sassari on the second-last Sunday in May to remember a decisive victory over the Arabs in AD 1000. Many will wear historic costumes.

## Il Palio della Balestra (Crossbow Competition)

This is a crossbow contest which takes place on the last Sunday in May between the Umbrian town of Gubbio and nearby San Sepolcro. It dates back to the fifteenth century and competitors wear appropriate historic costumes. A repeat match is held on the first Sunday in September, this time in San Sepolcro.

## Il Palio delle Quattro Antiche Repubbliche Marinare (Regatta of the Four Ancient Maritime Republics)

Each May, the four former maritime republics of

Venice, Genoa, Pisa and Amalfi take part in a splendidly colourful procession of boats before competing with each other in races. The event is hosted by each republic in turn. It was Genoa in 2004 and will be Amalfi in 2005, Pisa in 2006 and Venice in 2007.

## Festa di San Giovanni (Feast of St John)

Despite being described as *calcio storico* (historic football), this Renaissance game bears almost no relation to today's football. If it is like anything, it is rugby and not much like that either. It is extremely violent, though, which is partially explained by the fact that it was developed in the sixteenth century as a form of military training. Three games are played in Florence on the 24th of June each year between teams of no particular size, dressed in historic costumes. The games last one hour each.

## Gioco del Ponte (Game of the Bridge)

The origins of this Pisan game on the last Sunday in June go back to the fifteenth century, when it was a good deal more violent. Nowadays, individuals from two teams, the *Mezzogiorno* (from the Pisan districts south of the River Arno) and the *Tramontana* (north of the river) compete against each other to push a seven-tonne trolley across to the other side of the bridge. There are currently six individual contests and the game is preceded by a parade in Renaissance-style armour and clothing.

## Il Palio di Siena (Horse Race of Siena)

Records of this dangerous bareback horse race in Siena stretch as far back as 1286. Twice yearly, on 2nd July and 16th August, ten horses, each from a *contrada* (district) in the city, compete for the *palio*, a specially made banner. Unlike other horse races, the horse is not disqualified if its rider falls off. Riderless horses have been known to win. Unsurprisingly, injuries to both horse and rider are common. Spectators wear the same medieval colours as the riders from their *contrada*. It is all over in a little over a minute.


## Ardia

Men ride horses around a track outside the town of Sedilo in Sardinia to the sound of gunfire and celebrate the victory of Emperor Constantine over Maxentius in AD 312. There is a nearby chapel dedicated to Constantine, but otherwise it's an obscure excuse for a party, especially given that the battle itself was in Rome. It takes place on 6th and 7th July.


## Festa del Redentore (Feast of the Redeemer)

Dating back to 1576, this feast on the third weekend in July gives thanks for the end of a plague which killed one in three Venetians. On the Saturday, locals take picnics out on their boats across the water to watch some truly magnificent firework displays. On the Sunday, there is a procession over a bridge of boats to the Chiesa del Redentore for a service.


## Festa di San Gennaro

On 19th September and 16th December, people gather in the cathedral of Naples to watch the blood of San Gennaro liquefy in its phial. It always does, miraculously.

# Markets

There's two things you should know about Italy: it is a nation of food lovers and a country that has built its history, culture and wealth through trade and commerce around the Mediterranean. Put those elements together and you have a recipe for some of the finest street markets in Europe. Most towns and villages will have food markets that put any you find in the UK or US to shame for quality, choice and presentation.

## Campo dei Fiori

You find the most famous markets in the cities. None is better known than that of **Campo dei Fiori** in Rome. This colourful marketplace is also a popular spot for photographers as it has so much character. The Campo isn't a big square and its lack of space is emphasized by the colourful spread of this popular market. Don't come expecting neatness and order, however. What's on the stalls may be immaculate, but the square itself and most of the people who come here tend to be casual, even scruffy, in appearance. This very old Roman market is open Monday to Saturday, 8am to

1pm. You can buy a wide range of goods, including flowers, but people really come for the food: fresh fish, meats, vegetables, herbs, brightly coloured spices and other delicacies. You will remember the sights and smells every time you order a meal in Rome. As a bonus, on one of the corners of the square there is probably the best bakery in Rome. Prices are not cheap, but the bread tastes amazing.

The Campo used to be a public execution place for centuries and at its centre is a statue of the Italian philosopher, Giordano Bruno, who was burned here at the stake as a heretic in February 1600. He was an extraordinary man, small of stature but extravagant in style – one contemporary said that he 'had a name longer than his body'. He believed that the Earth revolved around the Sun and that the universe might be infinite and ever-changing, not the static creation of the teachings of the Catholic Church. He was a brilliant

and enthusiastic debater but enjoyed pointing out his opponents' intellectual failings far too much. Debating at Oxford in 1583, he commented on the rudeness and ignorance of the resident academics. He lived in London for a few years as a guest of the French ambassador and there is a theory that he earned a little pocket money by spying on his host for Queen Elizabeth I!

## Other great markets in Rome include:
### Porta Portese (Via di Porta Portese, Rome)
Chances are you will find what you want here – whatever it is – at the biggest market in Rome. Sprawled out over several acres, it can be pretty exhausting to trawl your way through, especially if it's crowded, which it usually is. Still, there are plenty of bargains to be had, although as at any market, if you're a really serious bargain-hunter, try and get here as early as possible, preferably at 5am when it starts!

### Underground (Via Francesco Crispi 96, Rome)
This antiques and collectors fair is fun. Most of the traders aren't in it for the money, they are collectors themselves and their enthusiasm will rub off on you.

There is even a section dedicated to traders between the ages of 7 and 14! The market's name comes from its location in a car park between Via Sistina and Via Veneto.

## Other Markets Around Italy

You could fill a book with all of the regular markets held in Italy during the year – and even then you wouldn't have space for the enormous number which only occur once a year. One of the nicest is the **Fiera di Sant'Ambrogio** in Milan at the beginning of December. It's essentially a pre-Christmas market, with many of the things on sale designed to be Christmas presents. Not surprisingly, it has an unusual, festive feeling, made stronger by the fact that it coincides with the annual *Festa di Sant'Ambrogio* celebrations in honour of Milan's patron saint.

This being the centre of the Italian fashion industry, there are, of course, markets here solely dedicated to clothing and shoes. The biggest – and best – is the **Mercato di Viale Papiniano** (Viale Papiniano, Milan). This is Milan's largest market, with many bargains to be had if you have the patience to find them. It happens every Tuesday and Saturday mornings. There are also great deals to be had in the **Piazza dei Ciompi** at Florence's **Mercato delle Pulci** (Flea market), all day, every day. The best time to go is on the last Sunday of the month, when the market spills into the nearby streets and stalls pile up further with objects of every kind and every value – stretching surprisingly and untidily far back into Italian history.

The best market in Florence can be found in the **Piazza Santissima Annunziata** (6–7 September). It has a history that reaches back centuries and used to be the last opportunity for farmers to sell their produce before the arrival of winter – their success (or failure) meant either comfort or starvation for their families. They would leave their farms before dawn and make their way into the city, holding out lanterns before them to guide their path. Their plight is remembered in

the *Festa della Rificolona* that precedes the great market. It ends with a procession of Florentine children through the streets on 7 September, carrying their own lanterns made from candles and tissue paper.

In Venice, most major markets are held on or near the **Rialto**, which has been in use for just that purpose for over 1,000 years. A market here, said Elizabeth David, the great British food writer, is the most spectacular in Italy. The range of food on display at the regular Tuesday to Saturday markets is breathtaking, a kind of luxury in itself. It's not just the mouth-watering produce, all bathed in Venice's magical light, it's also the smells of the local dishes, cooked fresh and a delight to eat in the cool of morning. In fact, get here as soon after dawn as you can muster. This is especially true of the fish market alongside the Rialto on the Grand Canal. If you get there really early, you might see the fishermen setting out their catch straight from the sea as their forefathers have done for centuries.

A sense of history hangs over many of Italy's greatest markets. Take **Il Mercato della Vucciria** in Palermo on Sicily, for example, which takes place daily in the narrow winding streets of the city's Arab quarter near Piazza San Domenico. Here it feels more like North Africa than Europe. Working your way through the thronging alleys you can stop at the *friggitorie* (little fry shops) and taste the deep-fried vegetables and rice balls, or see sea-fresh squid and octopus being lifted off smoking, spitting grills and placed on warm bread as a savoury snack to eat while you take everything in.

# A Little Bit
# of Sport

**O**ne word: football. Actually, that should be *calcio*, but you know what we mean. The Italians are mad for it – they call it 'the beautiful science'. You really haven't experienced live football until you've seen a top-flight game in *Serie A* (Premier League), especially in a stadium like San Siro in Milan.

The Italian football season starts in August and ends with the Italian Cup final in June, although there is a short break in the schedule around the New Year. Most matches are played on Sunday afternoons.

The Italian league has four divisions – *Serie A*, *Serie B*, *Serie C1* and *Serie C2*. As you would expect, it is *Serie A* that has the stellar international teams. There are 18 of them in *Serie A* each year, with the bottom four being relegated to *Serie B* at the end of the season. The reality is, though, that a handful of teams dominate. In recent times, it is a rare year when Juventus or Milan are beaten to the trophy. As in much of Italian life, the wealth and success remains in the north.

The leading clubs in *Serie A* are:

☞ **Inter**

Founded in 1908, InterMilan has never been out of *Serie A*. Its stadium is one of the greatest in the world and was originally built by Piero Pirelli, the legendary tyre manufacturer.

### ☞ Juventus

Nicknamed *La Vecchia Signora* (The Old Lady), Juventus was founded in 1897 and borrowed its black and white stripes from Notts County in 1903. (Before that, they played in pink.) It has never been out of *Serie A*.

### ☞ Lazio

Founded in 1900, Lazio shares its stadium – built for the 1960 Olympics – with fellow Roman club Roma.

### ☞ Milan

Somewhat surprisingly, Milan started out as the Milan Football and Cricket Club in 1899. Less surprisingly, it was founded by an Englishman and shares its stadium with Inter.

### ☞ Roma

Not born until 1927, Roma shares its stadium with fellow Roman giant Lazio. Perhaps surprisingly, it has only won the Championship three times.

### ☞ Sampdoria

A relative newcomer, this Genoese club wasn't formed until 1946. Despite some grim years in *Serie B*, especially in the

1970s, there is no doubt
that this is one of the
great football clubs in the world.

## Grand Prix

This is the country that gave the world
Ferrari and Maserati, not to mention
the more humble Fiat. Motor racing
is in its blood. The best place to
witness this obsession is at one of the
two Grand Prix in Italy, since you're
much less likely to get run over here
than elsewhere! Monza, the great
racetrack just outside Milan, was one
of the very first to host a race called
Grand Prix, in 1922. The Italian
Grand Prix is still held here every year, usually in
September. The San Marino Grand Prix at Imola tends
to be in April.

## Giro d'Italia

Less well known than the Tour de France, the *Giro
d'Italia* is a similar marathon test of cycling endurance.
This year's, for instance, will start in Genoa, take a brief
detour into Croatia and Slovenia before working its way
down the Adriatic Coast and then back up to Milan. It
will cover over 3,219 km (2,000 miles) in 20 days.

# Odds
# and Ends

## High Heels

Next time your parents whine about how ridiculous fashions are these days, tell them that in sixteenth-century Venice, some women wore shoes called *zoccoli* – which were essentially mules on 20-inch platforms. Gentlewomen couldn't actually go out without two maids to support them wherever they went. One visitor commented that the Rialto was 'full of dwarves transformed into giantesses'.

In the early twentieth century, one of the greatest and most influential of all Italian designers, Elsa Schiaparelli, carried on this tradition of flamboyance by designing hats that looked like boots and veal cutlets and using fabrics that looked like newsprint.

## Blessed Be the Coffee-Makers

At one point in history, religious fanatics were suspicious of coffee because it was known to be a stimulant and they believed that it encouraged bad behaviour. There were even moves afoot inside the Vatican to stamp out people drinking it altogether. The plan got as far as Pope Clement VII. (We have met him before: it was his misfortune to be pope when the Holy Roman Emperor Charles V sent his army to sack Rome in 1527.) 'Coffee,' his advisors told him 'is Satan's latest trap to catch Christian souls.' Clement asked to sample some before making a decision. He liked it so much that he baptized it, saying that it was so good it would be shame if only infidels could drink it!

## Who Said That Art Was Dead?

The great Renaissance painter Andrea del Sarto artist made himself a model temple using sausages as pillars and parmesan cheese for the base. But today's artists can use the most up-to-date technology to express their creativity. No one is more original than the artist known only as Stefano. Just 23, Rome-born Stefano has already found his mission in life: on 17 January 2003, he set up an Internet website called Pasta Log, where he keeps a record of every pasta meal he has ever eaten. The pasta he eats must be photographed at the start of every meal. So far, he has eaten 0.890410958904 bowls of pasta a day!

## Catacombe dei Cappuccini

(Catacombs of the Capuchins)

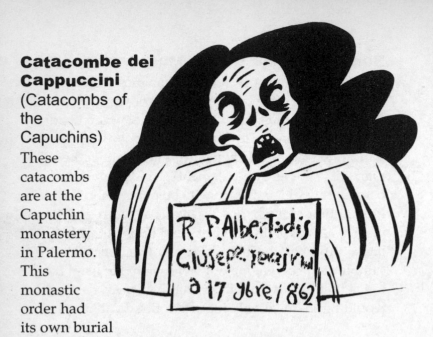

These catacombs are at the Capuchin monastery in Palermo. This monastic order had its own burial ground for around 500 years up until around 1881. Instead of burying their dead, the Capuchins preserved the bodies and stored them away in the maze of catacombs underneath the church.

The techniques for preserving bodies included the use of arsenic and vinegar baths, and they produced mixed results and varying degrees of success – as you can see for yourself. Eugh!

What makes matters really weird is that every body is dressed in his or her Sunday best. Each corpse also has its own niche in the wall, with a handwritten note hung around the neck explaining who they were. It's really, really ghoulish!

A word of warning: the catacombs are genuinely scary and are definitely not for the faint-hearted. And don't even think of going if you've just eaten!

# Emergency Phrases

## The Essentials

| | |
|---|---|
| Hi | *Ciao* |
| Hello | *Salve* |
| Goodbye | *Arrivederci* |
| Yes | *Si* |
| No | *No* |
| Where? | *Dove?* |
| When? | *Quando?* |
| Why? | *Perché?* |
| What? | *Che cosa?* |
| Who? | *Chi?* |
| Which? | *Quale?* |
| How? | *Come?* |
| How much? | *Quanto?* |
| How many? | *Quanti?* |
| Is there? | *C'è?* |
| Are there? | *Ci sono?* |
| Congratulations! | *Congratulazioni!/Felicitazioni!* |
| Happy Birthday! | *Buon Compleanno!* |
| Merry Christmas! | *Buon Natale!* |

| | |
|---|---|
| Happy New Year! | *Buon Anno!* |
| Happy Easter! | *Buona Pasqua!* |
| Good luck! | *Buona fortuna!* |
| Enjoy the meal! | *Buon appetito!* |
| Have a good holiday! | *Buone vacanze!* |
| I am sorry | *Mi dispiace* |
| I don't understand | *Non capisco* |
| Please | *Per piacere/per favore* |
| Thank you (very much) | *Grazie (mille)* |
| Excuse me | *Mi scusi* |
| May I? | *Posso?* |
| Of course | *Certamente* |

## About You

| | |
|---|---|
| My name is... | *My chiamo...* |
| I am twelve years old | *Ho dodici anni* |
| I am British (boy) | *Sono britannico* |
| I am British (girl) | *Sono britannica* |
| I am Irish (boy/girl) | *Sono irlandese* |
| I am American (boy) | *Sono americano* |
| I am American (girl) | *Sono americana* |
| I live in ... | *Abito a ...* |

## Food and Drink

| | |
|---|---|
| I would like a lemonade, please | *Vorrei una limonata, per favore* |

| | |
|---|---|
| Ice cream | *Il gelato* |
| Hot chocolate | *La cioccolata calda* |
| Chocolate cake | *La torta al cioccolata* |
| What sandwiches do you have? | *Che tipi di tramezzini ha?* |
| What flavours do you have? | *Che gusti ha?* |
| What do you recommend? | *Che cosa mi consiglia?* |
| I am a vegetarian (boy) | *Sono vegetariano* |
| I am a vegetarian (girl) | *Sono vegetariana* |

## Making Friends

| | |
|---|---|
| How are you doing? | *Come va?* |
| Where do you want to go? | *Dove vorresti andare?* |
| We'd like to see some football | *Vorremmo vedere una partita di calcio* |
| Sorry, I'm not free | *Mi spiace, non sono libero/a* |
| Maybe next week | *Forse la settimana prossima* |
| That would be great! | *Sarebbe fantastico!* |
| How about going to the cinema? | *Cosa ne dici di andare al cinema?* |
| What's on? | *Cosa fanno?* |
| I've already seen it | *L'ho già visto* |
| Is it subtitled? | *Ha sottotitoli in inglese?* |
| How long does the film last? | *Quanto è lungo il film?* |
| When does the film end? | *A che ora finisce il film?* |
| What is your name? | *Come ti chiami?* |
| Do you speak English? | *Parli inglese?* |
| I don't understand Italian | *Non capisco l'italiano* |

What do you call this in Italian?

*Come si chiama questo in italiano?*

| | |
|---|---|
| How old are you? | *Quanti anni hai?* |
| Where are you from? | *Di dove sei?* |
| Where do you live? | *Dove abiti?* |
| What is your telephone number? | *Qual'è il tuo (suo) numero di telefono?* |
| Do you have Playstation™? | *Hai una Playstation™?* |
| See you tomorrow? | *Ci vediamo domani?* |
| See you soon | *A presto* |

## ...And the Most Useful Phrase in Any Language

| | |
|---|---|
| Where's the toilet? | *Dov'è il bagno?* |

# Good Books

Heather Amery and Stephen Cartwright, *First Thousand Words in Italian* (Usborne)

Terry Deary, *The Rotten Romans* (Scholastic)
History with all the funny bits left in.

Marco Polo, *Travels of Marco Polo* (Penguin)
Decide for yourself whether he made it all up or not!

Silver (Guido Silvestri) *Il Grande Lupo Alberto* (Rizzoli)
But you will see loads of comics on news-stands, too

Geronimo Stilton, *Lost Treasure of the Emerald Eye* (Scholastic)
A huge hit in Italy, these are now being published in the UK for the first time. There are loads more!

Giorgio Vasari, *The Lives of the Artists (Oxford World Classics)*
All about the great artists of the Renaissance by someone who was there! (And the first book of art history, too.)

A. Wilkes and J. Shackell, *Italian for Beginners* (Usborne)

Philip Wilkinson, *What The Romans Did For Us* (Pan Macmillan)
Find out why the Romans were so successful in this book accompanying the TV series.

# Wicked Websites

**www.mappy.it**
More maps than you could possible want!

**www.uffizi.firenze.it**
One of the great museums and art galleries of the world.

**www.italiantourism.com**
Website of the Italian Tourist Board.

**www.meteo.it**
Where the Italians go online for their weather forecast.

**www.galleria.ferrari.com**
A museum dedicated to perhaps the world's finest cars.

**www.channel4.com/sport/football_italia**
The best English website about Serie A.

**www.worldinfozone.com**
Lots of interesting facts and useful information about Italy.

**http://www.blueflag.org/Map_Italy.asp**
Where to find Italy's cleanest beaches.

**www.italiansrus.com**
Italian life and culture in a single website. Includes a trivia quiz based on *Who Wants to be a Millionaire?*

**www.parks.it**
Every park in Italy – including upcoming events.

# Quirks and Scribbles